Dear Louis

May the words in this
book bless your heart ♥♥

Biggest love from

Channele Meliane Amawi

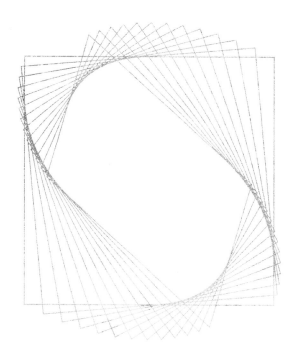

The Crystal Children Prophecies

CHANNELED BY

CHANNELE MELIANE AMAWI

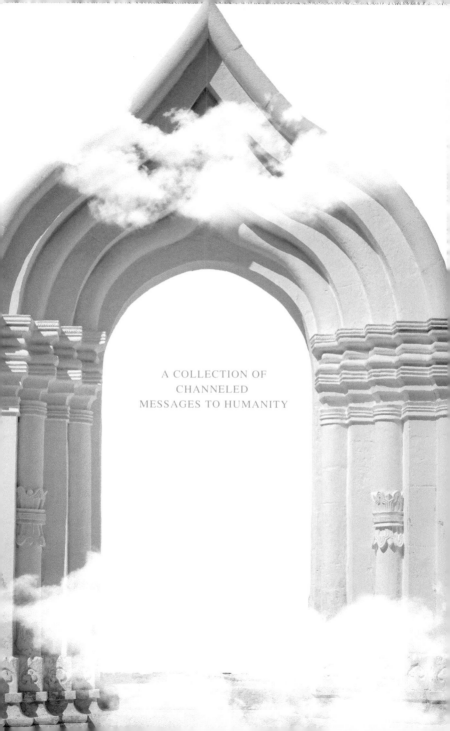

A COLLECTION OF
CHANNELED
MESSAGES TO HUMANITY

The Crystal Children Prophecies

TABLE OF CONTENTS

FOREWORD page i

I didn't know what channelling was until the words you are now holding in your hands flowed through me.

It all started back in 2009 when I went to Brazil on a two month journey to study with my mentors. This was one of the most intense initiations of my life. I was in my early twenties and eager to study within the spiritual disciplines. Back then I had no idea what that actually would mean, and what kind of journey that would take me on.

I was told on an earlier pilgrimage to India by a reputable Vedic astrologer that I would find great treasures in Brazil connected to my spiritual awakening, so I knew it would be of importance for me to go there.

During my stay with my spiritual mentors I went through continual training and deeper initiations into spiritual mystery traditions. I would be in deep states of meditation and immerse myself into ceremonies where I tapped into higher dimensions.

I had personal and direct experiences of God source and was shown how life came to be on this planet. I could see into the future and the past, throughout the ages and cycles where I was taken all the way back to the creation of this planet.

I was shown how to jump out of time and how to move through space without the limitations of the mind.

At one point one of the masters I was studying with taught me how to astral project my soul into the universe in a safe and guarded way, as this should not be done without supervision. My soul traveled around to different star systems in our galaxy. I had heard about astral travels before, but only through books.

I was now getting a first-hand experience of it myself. It was not that I learned so many new things, it was more that I was starting to remember who I truly was, where we all come from, and that before body, we are timeless souls connected to the entirety and eternity of the cosmos.

I came back to Sao Paulo in-between these profound spiritual initiations and insights with my teachers in the forest.

I was staying with a friend in a house near the city. Exhausted from the months of deep ceremonial work in the forest, I collapsed into bed.

Early next morning, before the sun had fully broken the dawn, I was dreaming about heaven. You know those dreams that are so real and vivid, they don't feel like a dream? It was one of those. I saw big, beautiful elephants in a parade, and people were riding on them while smiling and celebrating joyfully.

Within the dream I could hear bird song from outside my bedroom. The song of the birds pulled me up from my bed and I soon found myself standing in the garden. Their song pulled me upwards through the ethers, into the celestial and heavenly realms. I was bathing in light, drifting between worlds, called to the upper dimensions.

As I took a few more steps, I fell really hard down a small set of stone stairs in the garden. While I was laying there, I thought to myself; "If I don't ground myself after all these intense weeks of energy work, I might really hurt myself."

When your light being travels the stars and connects to the higher realms and realities, it is always important to ground down into Terra, into earth and the physical body afterwards, and I was far from grounded.

I walked back into the house through another door and found myself standing in the living room. Everyone else in the house was still asleep but I was not alone.

As I was standing there, still a little bit dazed, a quiet voice within told me,

"Go over to the bookshelf." I was a guest in this house and didn't know much about where anything was. The voice whispered to me again, "Put your hand behind the books." Reaching behind the row of Portuguese books, my hand landed on what looked like sheets of papyrus scrolls.

They were empty and looked ancient, and next to them, as if placed there, was a pen. I picked up both.

The voice then told me to go over to the sofa and sit down, and so I descended heavily into the cushions. Then the voice said, "Go to bed."

I watched my energy body go to bed. My physical body though, was still sitting in the living room. Now a benevolent being was occupying my body. This being was much larger than me. It was around two meters tall and wide, and with an equally large energetic presence.

This being then unrolled the dusty, brittle scrolls and began to write. And it wrote and it wrote. I would hear a loud voice echoing the words as they found their way down onto the scrolls.

This went on for days. I'd be in situations where out of nowhere, the channelled messages would continue to pour through.

Scrambling to find a pen and paper so as not to miss a word, I would stop and write. The messages would hit me like morse code. Often at inconvenient times. I wrote out several pieces of small paper notes that I had to then puzzle and piece together. I was shown powerful visions and revelations connected to the messages that were coming through.

Prior to this, I had never written anything in English except for a few class assignments as a child, while going to school in Norway. But to write this many poems that all rhyme in English? This was well and truly beyond my ability. I believe I was only able to do this because it was not me writing these words. They were channelled.

These words came through me but are not by me. Just as one would turn on a tap and let the water flow from it, so did the words flow out through me. This is the work you are now holding in your dear hands.

I would through the channeling discover that the spirit-being I connected with was more than one being.

This collective of beings called themselves Nostradamus. They presented themselves in different forms.

Illustrated and accompanied by vivid visions while I received these prophetic messages, I was shown what will happen to our Earth in the distant future. I saw a whole new continent that would spring up from the Atlantic Ocean in between Europe and America, among many other visions.

I was shown how civilizations will thrive under the sea in the future and how pain and darkness will be a distant memory of the past. I was taken all the way back to how life on this Earth started and how every time the universal mind thinks a thought, a whole new galaxy, world or species appears.

What you are about to read are coded messages to humanity, and they provide great guidance on how we can live our lives in more harmony, strength, and in full surrender that we are held by the divine.

What I've come to realize through "The Crystal Children Prophecies" is that we are dearly loved by the divine. May this work serve as a great reminder of your divinity and soul essence, as well as how much you are loved by Creator Source.

"The Crystal Children Prophecies" is truly a love letter from the Divine.

I highly recommend taking your time reflecting upon these coded messages and bathe in the vibratory frequency hidden between these words as they will be working with you on a deep level.

Oceans of love from the one heart of creation.

Morning Star

CHAPTER 1

Morning star
shine bright for me tonight
Light up our path
so we may see clear
Light up my path
so I may come near

Sing me the song
that I once knew
In the starry vast sky
all I see is you

Take me home
to the golden fields
and my throne
There always to remember
my true heart song

Morning Star

Silence is the song
where I will awake
Crossing all the bridges
that I know I must take

The throne is golden blue
the golden bridge
will take you through
There never to forget
your true heart song

My name is love
and I have no form
Since my formlessness
is the only thing I know

The ring is magic
and it's easy to fall in love
Watch out
there is a danger
in spacing out

❃

The view is clear
and you are so near
Preparing the road for
generations to go

You are the treasure
you always were
and you will always be
The treasure of within
lies in humanity

Knowing I will come
when the time has come
So now remember sweet child
remember your heart song

﹡

If you only knew my desire
to fill you with all that you need
If you only knew my home is open
whenever you want to come home

If you only invited me to
the party I would come

Releasing you from this pain
that you have known so long
I wish to whisper in your ear

That I am here
I am near
So now dear child
have no fear

❋

My name is indeed Love
and I have no form
Since formlessness
is the only thing I know

From the beginning of creation
I belong to all

I can get very small
and also very tall
Do you remember sweet child
the tall is small is all

Waiting for the coast to be clear
guarding you from fear
Receiving all that is here

Singing your song
while you go along
Precious lovely gemstone

❋

Morning Star

Reaching love
In your temple of home
Imagining a world
where you will be heard

Laying in the ditch
and then release the third

Smelling the flowers
that I once gave to you
Reaching the love throne
that I once gave to you

So now don't be afraid
of what next I have to say

❋

Love is a mystery
where you no longer have to take
Putting yourself at stake
don't be afraid of a mistake

You are not lonely anymore
you are in safe shores

I really want to help
so now you know you are in my place
Really wanting you to take care
of your heart so precious dear

Now have no fear
and tell your generations near
that it's all already here

Rainbow Heart

CHAPTER TWO

Rainbow Heart

Golden green and yellow blue
new colored spectrums appearing too
The crystal children are coming through

Rainbows at their heart
they don't know how to fight
Bringing home your light

Be brave now little one
and I will sing you a new song
About a reborn star full of light
surely singing out the night

Ringing in a new day
that will make you want to stay
I will come upon this earth to show
what you all already know

※

Now protecting you from the last grip
you know you have to sink the ship
Then there is only light
and finally I will shut my mouth

Knowing I will come
when the iron ship is down

Bye bye now
casting out all the gear
That's unnecessary here

Reaching for the blue within
that's now shining through your skin

God is actually right here
so now you only have to dis-appear

*

Rainbow Heart

I wish to breathe
upon this Earth again
But then it could be
you have to swim

Of golden colored
light ahead
A crystal light
could easily spread
And then goodbye
to the dead

Rebirth is coming near
so get prepared
To cut the cord

You already have
the golden sword
To cut all that's left
of hatred, pain and all the rest

Winning is such fun
when you know that there is only one

✳

The crystal ship
will now appear
So listen to
the golden reindeer

Knowing you don't
have to try so hard
Knowing that I'm here
And everywhere

Light was never in your hand
for you to go and shut them down
Please don't misunderstand

Listening to the voice within
there I will call you by your name
When the bells ring in
don't be afraid to win

Crystal ship is my name
I come in the colors of the rain
I don't really have a name

I am one with the crystal sky blue
bringing new generations through
Crystal ship is coming through

❋

Rainbow Heart

The Virgin Ship

Now welcoming the virgin ship
taking her journeys through
Galaxies so blue

Here she will always stay
bringing in the force of horse

Receiving her knowing
there won't be loss
Realizing there is no cost
to liberation if you want to cross

Knowing God already set you free
when the time comes you will see

※

Wishing you will listen
to the little reindeer
Singing her song
of the love that is to come

Science is a myth
where you can lose your grip
So don't hold too tight
and no more need to fight
The temple is in the knight

Wishing you to remember
why we at all fight
It's all just for the flight
so don't hold too tight

❈

Rainbow Heart

If you dig in the mountain Moria
you will find the rest of Lemuria
Just be careful so you don't awake
a creature red like a snake

Lemuria is at your door
of this you can be quite sure
The dolphins playing along
the great earth song

The Return of Her

CHAPTER THREE

Of the Return of Her

Pro-hence I will tell you a story hoping you will not forget

※

Now I want to sing you the song of the sea
that I will sing upon this Earth eons to be

Love is my name
steeped in the fundament of this Earth
The ships are coming home

❋

In the beginning
there was blood
And in the end
it will be red again

In the middle
it was blue
Quite clear too
fields of golden barley
and there were fishes too

Snakes in the grass
and horses on the terrace

And then Eve came along
and she sung her song
Mating with her love
feeling quite at home

❋

The Return of Her

Lonely as they were
content they were not
So children they had a lot

Love was not their game
so they went off spot
Creating many knots

Losing in their game
then along came the blame
And shame

✳

Of wanting to release a big burden
God released the herdsman
They spoke and they whispered
but it all got twisted

God shook his head
releasing the dead

Now was the time
where the lions came aside
They knew the time was short
and quickly as they walked
Deus released his wandering chalk

✳

The Return of Her

Bella Rosa

Listening to the wind
Bella Rosa wished to swim
Released from the dagger
she gasped for air
And the fisherman finally
disappeared

Waiting for her groom
knowing the coast was clear

Sea and Earth merged again
old lovers were their dream
And then love ruled again

*

Listening to the wind
Bella Rosa now could swim
Finally doing her thing
playing in the grass

Drinking from the glass
singing her song
Of what's already known

Knowing it's all gold
and it's all given
If you don't hold

So then the sky met the Earth
and gave a rebirth
To a new sun
and the song began

✳

The Return of Her

Sun king was his name
he couldn't wait to rule again
Waiting for her to arrive
so they could have another child

Now listening to the wind
Bella Rosa could finally swim
married to the golden king

And she will sing her song
until the days come along
When two is known as One

❄

Golden

City

Throne

CHAPTER
FOUR

Listening to the wind
Bella Rosa wished to swim
Her belly getting blue
the prophet is coming through

Crystal child so blue
Krishna is coming through
So now kissing your baby boy
the dear product of your story told

❁

Ayodhya is coming near
in the middle of the Dead Sea
the new beginning you can see

Reaching high above
Ramana's kingdom hold

Ramana is the blue sun
that will guide you home

You don't have to fear
what is coming near
It's all already here

✳

The golden city is so near
so dear child of mine have no fear

Crystalizing from within
the secrets of the Maya Queen
That was hiding there for a while
but is now ready to be your guide

Now whispering in your ear
of what is coming near
You don't have to fear

For loving is such a throne
in which all is coming home
Leaving none

Finally grasping for air
now without fear

Loving what is real
and yet without no deal
To seal or behold
for this love can't behold
nor sold - only told

To the one who can receive
the golden-bridged wheel
Of love light and existence
how could it get so twisted?

Only for you to remember
the gold is already in your temple

*

Realizing from within
the secrets of the Maya King

Reaching for the lovely gold
that's already sold
If you only make the call

Now reaching out your lovely hand
releasing the old sand
And I will give you the sacred land
that's already in your hand

Now reaching for all the gold
that's already sold
Only for the next on the road

What next I have to say is clever
that drinking from the wine is heaven
The wine is drunken right here right now

So don't be afraid to shine
Rainbow Child of mine

*

Nostradamus is coming through
and he is she to guide you
To make you understand
the treasure is in your hand

Taking you through
to the treasure of me and you

Morning star is clear and blue
I am here to guide you
On the road so bumpy
I will make it less humpy

Listening to the voice within
that will guide you too
The treasure shoe

※

Now all you have to do
is drink the vine of the spine
And I will guide you through

Knowing I will come
to bring home
all children of mine
To the golden city throne
sweet sun child come home

So golden children
get rid of the burden
that you held so dear
Burning it on the cross
where I appeared

❄

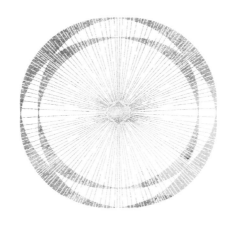

Why was this night so cool
for you to miss the Golden school

The school from high up above
where you will graduate
with all your loves

So now open your eyes
And get rid of all the lies
that awoke high up in the skies

❄

Golden City Throne

Nectar from the Sun

CHAPTER FIVE

I have a thousand endless names
But they are all really the same

Nectar from the Sun

Now I want to tell you the story
once whispered in the sun
That you no longer need to run
because time is just another myth
That doesn't really exist

Knowing the days will come
where you no longer have to run
Drinking the nectar from the sun
giving you all the keys you need
To the golden castle indeed

Now praying for you dear child of mine
that you will reach far and high
I am sitting in the flower tower
there I will rest within my chest

Waiting for you to surely win
back the lost queen
Then I'm waiting for you
to knock on my door
There to rest for to evermore

Oi, order in the hall
Don't mean to be reluctant
it's all because you didn't listen
Someone had to put the border
or else it wouldn't be in order

"Yes ma'am"
is the next command

Order is my name
I don't own any shame
since I don't have
Anyone to blame

Come on why wait
when loving is at stake

Telling you I will shake
if you don't make it
To the water lake

Listening to the star within
that's lying at the virgin queen
The blessing of miss Quan Yin
so now kiss her feet
While you give her your crying sheet

Singing your song
while you go along
My precious lovely gemstone

Praying for you
dear child of mine
That you will reach far and high

The white snake is here
to show you truth
And assist you through
really know it will guide you

❊

Trust is the greatest task
so please just ask
For help when you need
and you will receive

Listening to the eagles tear
of what is about to come here
Is easy to understand
when you're in the sacred land

In the pyramids you can see
a clue of the old deed
Their ways are not right
so make sure to cast them out

Nectar from the Sun

Golden Star

Once upon a time
there was a star
In the desert of Sahar

The Sun shone
and the rain came down
From starry sky so blue
sunlight reaching through

The green was golden blue
many stars coming through

The Golden Star was shining there
in many spectrum colors clear
Singing more of the tears of gold

Listening to the star within
that shines through your skin
Bright is the star in your eye
so hold on while you're going home
Speeding up and then we're done

✻

Crystal Gardens

CHAPTER SIX

The Rose is blooming
deep within
The breath of Deana
can be seen

He drowned her head
completely in the water lake
Her head fell on the ocean floor
there it lay until the dawn

Crack appeared in ocean ground
red and naked
Making noises everywhere

Her head finally appeared
in the sand far on the sea ground

She knew it wouldn't take a lot of time
until the star would come down
So she once again could breathe
and show her smile for a while

Swinging her hips around
without it being like a crime
That you would be punished for
and looked upon like a whore

✳

She really couldn't wait
to once again awake
In the hearts of everyone
she knew it would be a lot of fun

Finally she could be free
forever in eternity
Enough of hatred and twisted love
she was ready to swim up above

Crystal gardens appearing where
her foot touches on every sphere
Now all you need is to receive
and she will help you see clear

Deana was her true name
breathing out creation came
Call on her and she will help
the one who's trapped in oneself

Crystal Gardens

Now singing her song once more
make sure to put flowers at her door
And she will appreciate
and show you to your true self

If you cross the sea
you will finally see
What this Earth
was really meant to be

A paradise in disguise
just so you could get it right

She is really returning here
bringing in new learning
Have faith dear
and you will defeat fear

❄

Silver Water Spring

Receiving the water of the chalice
receiving the blessing from the water queen
The silver water spring
there I will cast out all fear
Bringing in new hope here

So now listen to what I have to say
you are my dear water lake
What I'm here about to say
is that you don't have to break

The holy thread
of the sacred water lake
It's all in the DNA
the secrets of the forest veil

I am wishing to arise
casting out all disguise
I'm happy to be a guiding flashlight

❄

Up in the mountain high
you will find a piece of the sky
In the mountain deep
you will find a virgin asleep

She is waiting for you to call
her energy into this world
She only comes when you knock
so please don't stop

Up in the mountain blue
you can find a virgin clue
Knowing I will come and awake
when the world is at stake

The snake is no longer
an enemy to me
He is my friend to be
so then we made love
Out on the blue sea

❀

Crystal Gardens

He put my legs back on
so I could walk my love song
In every woman upon this earth so
I could finally have a rebirth

Far up in Alaska
and in the Himalayas too
The skeletons will
finally come through

Channeling the guards
of the milky stars

So don't look too much outside
your heart is your true guide

Finally you arrive
putting your horse aside
Not wandering anymore
cause now you are in safe shores
And you don't exist anymore

※

Crystal Gardens

New Shores

They tried to steal
the golden copper wheel
Only so they could have a meal
but true beauty you can't digest

They tried to steal
the golden copper wheel
But stealing it you cannot
It's already in your heart

The new age will also bring new tears
that's why I am now here

I will never disappear
just call on me for help
And I will show you to yourself

Opening all the doors
that will take you to new shores

Bringing in the new Lord
and surely his Queen
Whose heart is pristine

Taking you back home
to the lovely golden throne

There to finally disappear
into the crystal water so clear

※

Crystal Gardens

This figure of eight
will disappear
But only if you share

This knowledge belongs to all
not only the tall
And the moment you hold
it only for yourself
You put it on the shelf

Don't listen to the Buddhist
who will tell you
you didn't exist
He will tell you you can't win
that you never had the right skin

✳

Finally you came home
it took some time
Seeing you smile
happy little child

Is it not very clear
what you are wishing for here?
So have no fear
Cause I am coming through
reaching out to you

I am here to guide you through
that's why we at all are two

✳

It's where dreams come alive
but they also quickly die
Knowing that death is just a test
Where you can finally get your rest

❋

Star of Hope

CHAPTER SEVEN

*The following sequence is a dialog between
a star named hope and a child seeking the
guidance of the star:*

*Now Hope could breathe again
finally doing her thing
Of blessing the ones
who are open to her star*

*Child:
"Why do you come so near,
when I don't want to disappear"*

*Star:
"Cause in truth
that's the only thing you seek*

*Change coming
I will bring
The treasure of
the God within*

*If you wish
I will surely come
Shining through
every single one"*

Star of Hope

Child:
"Come come come
I trust in God
I trust the guarding star
finally I'm home
Take me all the way through
all the way back to you"

Star:
"You deserve every ray of light
that is given in this night"

Child:
"Stay, stay forever with me
so I will always see
Take what's left of me
and help me cross this sea"

Star:
"Come nearer child
don't be afraid
This will burn a little
that's what it takes
Then you will feel ease
and finally be at peace"

The Crystal Children Prophecies

Star of Light

"This peace I'm singing
of here to you
Will finally bring you through
the mysteries of all that is

Receiving here is what it takes
for you to cross the water lake
The white bird will there appear
and you will finally see clear

Star of light is coming through
I've really been trying to reach you

I'm here to tell you
why at all we split in two

If you ever feel lonely
just call upon me
And I will protect you
and give you the nectar

I will come down
from the dark starry sky
The story may end here
so you may see clear

Appearing in the night sky
do you really know why?

I come here to bring my queen
so she can rule again

Casting out all fears
so you may see clear
I'm taking you home
to the golden throne

❊

The home is in your temple
may this message be protected
So we may stay connected

Now listening to me
about the story that is to be
You can direct
we choose the next step

I am here to purify the wound
that is in your chest

Amor is at the door
so just make sure
You're not laying on the floor

✻

Open your heart and you will find
the true treasure is in your spine
Changing the old code
that will take you on another road

Drinking from the wine of the spine
that will make you climb

Longing to see clear
through your heart dear
Finally everything's all right
accepting all in this night

I am shining bright and clear
so that you may come near
Trying to attract you home
so we may be at One."

Child:
"Dear star please sing to me,
of what my next step could be"

Star:
"Respecting all the elders
that put you in the cellar
They really didn't mean
to take the nectar
from within

So forgiving them is the clue in
which you will reach through

Jumping over the block
that made you have a stop
Releasing them from within
and you will surely win

❋

Star of Hope

Volcanoes will arise
but only to say goodbye
to all the hate inside

You don't have to fear
what is coming near
Volcanoes will arise
only to let out the spouse

Aggression is not an enemy
but a good friend to be
Welcoming all that you are
and then receive your star

Saying sorry is a glory
so now don't you worry

❋

I will always have a channel here
so now dear child have no fear
I will find my way through to you

The bird will appear when you're done
bringing home your love song
I will shine in my castle throne

Appearing in the night sky
There I will be for a while."

*

Star:
"Come closer dear
and I will appear"

Child:
"Please cut the cord
give me light
give me love"

Star:
"When you see it's in me
I will set you free

✳

The sought is in the seeker
so now it's no longer a secret

In the golden forest you are home
and the memory of pain is gone

Now sharing your light
with the ones who want

Amor does not fight."

*

Hope would arrive
in the night sky
Spreading her light
through the dark night

Do you know why?
She is here to give light
for the new rights

Bright and clear she is
wanting to give you a gift

※

Wanting you to know
why we are going home
Because the time has come
to let in the sun

Now don't you worry
about the new story
It will unfold
like every story told

The treasure is within
so now you know
you will surely win

What more can I say
that will make you awake?

❈

Child:
"I forgive myself
for all the actions I made
Knowing there is a new beginning
in where I will not carry
the wounds from the past
inside my precious heart

Now I will only work for this light
knowing it's all right
to not want to fight."

Star:
"So when the preacher is defeated,
knowing there is only teaching
and no preaching
I will be here to reach you."

❆

Never comparing yourself
with your friends
Is a key
that will set you free

. *Comparison*
will not take my throne
Love can't be measured in
big or small
Love is all

Remember me
and I will always be
In the hearts of the ones
who will give birth
to the new earth.

※

Star of Hope

If you want the story to continue
we just have to find a window

To look to space
will be your mistake
But you will surely learn
dear child of the sun

Now why are you so afraid
of what is here already said

I will not tell you anymore
until this knowledge here
is complete and sure

*

For filling your hearts with more
would be too much at your door

Now dear child
don't be mad at me
It was all just to make you see

Keeping it all to yourself
is the biggest mistake
Caring for your loved ones
is the only thing that truly counts."

❊

The Golden City

CHAPTER EIGHT

To Hornelius

Wishing you to see clear
through your heart dear
Reaching the golden mountain
within lies your garden

In the garden I will give
the nectar from my father

So please come home with me
and you will finally see
Why we went through
the treasure sea

I will never give up
that is my last call
Knowing that we will surely win
cause the nectar is already within

❋

Why did we go so far
all the way from Qatar
Only to find the treasure here
in the same sphere

Now looking in my deep blue eyes
knowing I will finalise
This journey right here
right now

So please don't go
for another ride

I will be stranded here
until you can see clear
I am waiting at the shores
of Avalon the boat will go

❋

The Golden City

So please lovely come home with me
and we will finally see
How it's all really meant to be

Two swans flying through the sun
is much better than one

Now my love for you is so strong
it's really drawing us back home
Back home to where we are from

The old country
and the sounds of the blowing horns

Wishing you to see so clear
that you already are so near
The golden city
where you're from
Please baby come back home

❄

Mona Lisa had a smile
that made you wonder for a while
Of what secrets she could hide
it all lies in the smile

※

The Pearlescent Princess

Pearl was her name
and she really could not blame
herself or the other

She was thinking
why do they even bother
when the treasure is at your heart?

So why did we even start
this funny game of hatred?
Only for you to get all naked

※

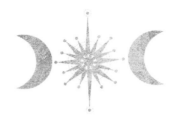

In the moon there comes a light
That is finished with her fight

Weapons lying at the floor
She doesn't want to fight anymore

So now asking you to lose your grip
at my throat so I can breathe

Let's be one once again
and may the story never end

The End

*Channel of The Crystal
Children Prophecies*

Channele Meliane Amaw

*"Just as one would turn on a tap
and let the water flow from it, s
did the words in
"The Crystal Children
Prophecies"
flow out through me.*

*I would through this channelea
work discover how much we are
deeply loved.*

*This book is truly a love letter
from creator source.
May it serve as a great reminde
of your divinity and spark the
remembrance of who
you truly are."*

*In love and light,
into the
One Heart of Creation!
Channele*

*Cover art by
Jeff Haynie
Book illustrations by
Isabelle Salem*

www.activatedangel.com
www.atalantia.com
channele@activatedangel.com
Instagram: _angel_sphinx